ECO

THRIFTY

ECO-THRIFTY

Text by Anna Martin

An Hachette UK Company
www.hachette.co.uk

Summersdale Publishers Ltd
Part of Octopus Publishing Group Limited
Carmelite House
50 Victoria Embankment
LONDON
EC4Y 0DZ
UK

www.summersdale.com

Printed and bound in the Czech Republic

Printed on paper from sustainable sources

ISBN: 978-1-78783-260-2

Substantial discounts on bulk quantities of Summersdale books are available to corporations, professional associations and other organizations. For details contact general enquiries: telephone: +44 (0) 1243 771107 or email: enquiries@summersdale.com.

ECO THRIFTY

Discover the Secrets to Stylish and Sustainable
Living Without It Costing the Earth

ALEXA KAYE

Disclaimer

Neither the author nor the publisher can be held responsible for any loss or claim arising out of the use, or misuse, of the suggestions made herein. Always follow the manufacturer's guidelines when using craft materials or chemicals with specific instructions and, if you have sensitive skin, protect your hands with rubber gloves.

CONTENTS

Introduction

We're all waking up to the catastrophic effects of human activity on the environment, from the world's polluted oceans and its sea life tainted with plastic, to the air pollution caused by mass production, deforestation and fossil fuels. We all want to do our bit, but sometimes it can be difficult to know where to begin.

Eco-Thrifty (made from sustainable papers and card!*) is the perfect companion to a more mindful approach to spending less and living more sustainably. Within these pages you will discover that it's not just about making do in order to reduce your impact on the environment – it's also about getting creative and being stylish too! Whether you take a pair of scissors to a favourite old dress that has seen better days and revamp it into a bespoke new skirt with a tuck here and a new fastening there, or you make use of the bruised fruit languishing in your fruit bowl to

rustle up something delicious, being eco-thrifty is about saying no to waste, saving money and enjoying the good things in life on a budget, and this guide – with tips on how to live inexpensively with an awareness of your carbon footprint – will show you how.

By the end of this book, you may find that you have a new mindset when it comes to thinking creatively about the waste you produce and how to maximize its uses while limiting your impact on the environment.

* Check out how to upcycle this book into a photo frame on page 38!

9

HOUSEHOLD AND DIY
Home is Where the Eco-Thrifty Heart is

There are many simple but effective ways of being eco-thrifty in your home, from the choices you make when buying furniture to reducing the products you purchase with single-use packaging. There are some fun and creative ways of being eco-thrifty too. Within this chapter you will discover how to make a simple piece of furniture out of reclaimed materials and an heirloom quilt from your favourite old T-shirts, as well as environmentally friendly ways to keep your house sparkling clean.

We're all aware of what can and can't be recycled, but once we've binned something, we often forget that we're not really getting rid of it: it's just being moved to somewhere else. Here's a timeline of the everyday products many of us use, showing how long they take to decompose.

Paper	2–5 months
Cotton T-shirt	6 months
Wool socks	1–5 years
Leather shoes	25–40 years
Nylon fabric	30–40 years
Tin cans	50–100 years
Aluminium cans	80–100 years
Styrofoam cup	500 years to forever
Plastic bags	500 years to forever
Glass bottles	1 million years

Every time you spend money, you are casting a vote for the kind of world you want.

Anna Lappé

Say "No" to the Dress... and Everyday Stuff You Don't Need

We can't go zero waste in an instant, but here are some very achievable quick wins which could dramatically reduce your waste production and consumer consumption.

- The best place to start is to consider what you really need, over what you'd like or desire. If you pose this question to yourself every time you have the urge to splurge, you'll soon discover that you can happily live with less.

- Identify what items you throw away on a regular basis and substitute them with reusable versions. For example, if it's coffee cups – we've all been guilty of this at some point – buy a refillable cup and take it with you EVERYWHERE. If it's packaging for sandwiches, use reusable wax wraps instead (see page 110 to learn how to make your own). If it's cotton pads for removing make-up, use reusable pads instead (see page 90 on how to create your own!). There are so many ways to be more eco-thrifty – and this book will show you how!

- Look at the things that you've bought recently that haven't really made you happy – like that dress with the irregular hem – and vow never to buy them again!

- Don't go to the supermarket when you're hungry (or hangry – that's even worse!) as you'll impulse buy snacks that are not only bad for you but tend to come in heaps of packaging, which is bad for the environment.

- Don't allow yourself to be tempted – stay away from the shops that seem to magically extract your cash before your rational mind has caught up with your irrational heart!

- Adopt a "one in, one out" policy to your belongings, be it clothing, books or ornaments, so you never increase the amount of stuff that you own.

- See the things that you buy as long-term investments – ask yourself what future you see for things before you buy them. Can you see yourself still treasuring them in six months, a year, five years or ten years from now?

- Look at the ethical policies of the companies that you buy from. There are companies cropping up everywhere that vow to limit their carbon footprint, from lingerie companies that will only use offcuts from the fashion industry, food companies that are plastic-free, coffee shops that are zero waste and furniture companies that plant trees to replace the ones that are felled for their products. Being eco-thrifty is about making intelligent choices, and with your support this ethical mindset will spread.

Keeping It Clean

Keeping your house clean is essential to avoid the build-up of hazardous bacteria and grime, and no one wants to live in a grubby house, after all. But these products that sanitize our surfaces and make our toilets smell nice often contain harmful levels of pollutants, including phosphorus, nitrogen and ammonia, which are highly toxic to animals and contribute to air and water pollution. These chemicals are not removed by waste treatment processes, and once absorbed by plant and aquatic life, the plants grow rapidly before decaying and contaminating the water, which is then no longer fit for human or animal use.

Here are some further reasons why you might want to reconsider using chemicals in the home:

- Current government legislation does not require manufacturers to list their ingredients on their product packaging.

- There are no mandatory safety tests carried out on cleaning products used in the home – so it's entirely up to manufacturers what they put into them.

- According to the Occupational Safety and Health Administration (OSHA), the average house has 50 times the "standard" level of exposure to chemicals.

After those bombshells, who wouldn't want to replace their cleaning products with ones that are safe and chemical-free, and ones that can be made very economically with products from the kitchen cupboard? Yes, please! Time to roll up your sleeves...

THE ECO-THRIFTY
CLEANING CUPBOARD

Kit out your cleaning cupboard with these products
and you'll never go back to bleach again!

Bicarbonate of soda	Available in large quantities from a chemist or pharmacy as opposed to the small pots in the baking aisle.
White vinegar	Available at the supermarket.
Lemon juice	Use the real thing!
Essential oils	Your house will smell delicious with just a few drops of essential oil, such as tea tree, lavender, eucalyptus and lemongrass – pick your favourite!
Castile soap	This is a vegetable-based soap, which is natural, non-toxic and biodegradable. It's available as a liquid or in a solid soap. It can be used as a deodorizing body wash and an all-purpose cleaner for your house!
Soapnuts	Despite being called "nuts", these are magical fruits containing saponin, a soap-like substance that is released on contact with water. They work in the same way as chemical detergents, but are chemical-free, completely natural, biodegradable and they're very effective at cleaning away grime. They can be bought from specialist suppliers online.
Soda crystals	These are what your great-gran would have used to do her laundry! They're an eco-thrifty dream as not only are they environmentally friendly, super cheap and available in all supermarkets, but they clean your clothes, remove limescale build-up in your machine as they soften the water and they also soften your clothes! They have other uses too, such as removing algae and moss from garden furniture.
Spare jars and spray bottles	When making your own products, you will need containers. Opt for glass or recyclable plastic that you can use again and again.

HOMEMADE WASHING-UP LIQUID

This simple mixture won't be as bubbly as the shop-bought liquids but it does the same job and is kinder to your skin.

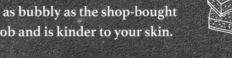

Ingredients

3 tbsp liquid Castile soap

0.25 l (0.4 pt) warm water

2 tbsp white vinegar

A few drops of pine or lavender essential oil*
(whichever oil you prefer, but these two have antibacterial properties)

Screw-cap or squeezy bottle

Method

Pour all of the ingredients into a screw-cap or squeezy bottle. Close the lid firmly and give it a good shake to mix well. When it comes to using it, squirt about a dessertspoon of the mixture into warm water and swirl with your hands.

* Be mindful of allergies if you choose not to wear washing-up gloves.

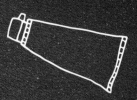

HOMEMADE TOILET CLEANER

Ban the bleach and use this fresh and fizzy
solution to keep your toilet clean.

Ingredients

100 g bicarbonate of soda

250 ml white vinegar

A few drops tea tree oil

A few drops pine essential oil

Jar (a jam jar will suffice)

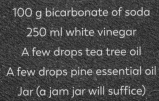

Method

When it's time to freshen up the toilet, mix the bicarbonate
of soda with the essential oils in a jar. Pour in the active
ingredient, the white vinegar, which will react with the
bicarbonate of soda, making it fizzy and ready to use. Pour the
mixture around the toilet bowl and leave it to do its thing!

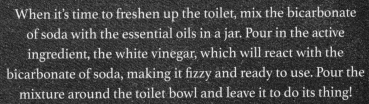

HOMEMADE ALL-PURPOSE DISINFECTANT

For cleaning surfaces and worktops, this recipe contains some of the same ingredients as the toilet cleaner but in different amounts.

Ingredients

250 ml white vinegar

1 tbsp bicarbonate of soda

1 l (1.75 pt) hot water

Juice and rind of half a lemon or lime (as preferred)

Spray bottle

Method

Mix the white vinegar, bicarbonate of soda and hot water in a large bowl or bucket. Squeeze the juice of your lemon or lime into the mixture and pop in the rind for good measure. Decant the liquid into your spray bottle (minus the rind!) and it's ready to use in the same way as any other all-purpose cleaner.

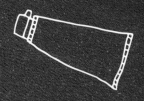

HOMEMADE WINDOW CLEANER

Vinegar, newspaper and a bit of elbow grease are
all you need for a perfect shine!

Ingredients

250 ml white vinegar
2 l (3.5 pt) warm water
Spray bottle
Newspaper

Method

This couldn't be easier as it's a mix of one part vinegar
to eight parts water. Decant the liquid into a spray
bottle ready to squirt your windows. Use a squeegee
blade to remove the excess liquid and an old newspaper
as a polishing cloth for a streak-free shine.

Quick Eco-Thrifty Household Tips

Restore your favourite teacup to its former glory by rubbing salt into stubborn stains with a sponge. Rinse, smile and put the kettle on for a fresh brew.

There's no need for expensive silver polish. Instead try rubbing a banana skin on silver for a brilliant shine.

To remove wax from carpeting, use an ice cube to encourage the wax to become cold and hard. Next, use a soft-edged spatula or a credit card to scrape up as much of the wax as you can. Place some paper towels over the affected area, turn on the iron to a low heat setting, and place it on the towels. As the wax softens up because of the heat, the paper towels will become saturated. Lift up the iron to make sure that the wax has not soaked all the way through so that there is no damage to the iron. Repeat the process until all the wax has been removed.

Make your own furniture polish: grate beeswax into a heatproof container, add turpentine and heat over a pan of water until the beeswax dissolves. Add a few drops of natural oil, such as lavender. Once cooled, apply to furniture with a soft cloth and buff to a sheen.

Sustainable Furniture

It's nice to have new furniture, and today you can kit
out your place relatively inexpensively due to mass
production, but think carefully before you commit to making
a purchase and do a bit of investigating as to the ethical and
environmental practices of the companies that you buy from.

Of course, the biggest impact of furniture production is
deforestation. Trees are vital for reversing climate change.
You might think it won't make a difference if you buy
a new table and set of chairs, but if we all thought
like that, there would be no trees left!

Repair, Restore, Upcycle

Before purchasing new, think of all the old furniture out there, the preloved tables and chairs that find their way to second-hand stores and online auction sites – you could even call it "vintage" to make it sound more appealing! There are many outlets that sell second-hand furniture nowadays, and with a bit of creative flair you can adapt your finds into something unique and truly special. Here are some ideas to whet your appetite for upcycling furniture.

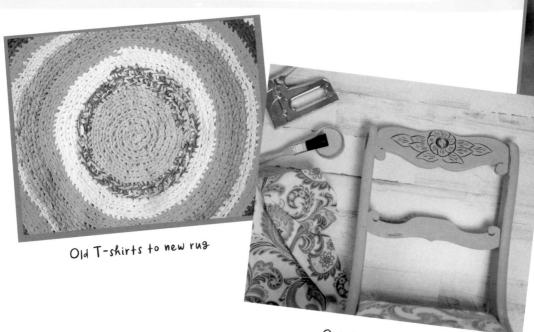

Old T-shirts to new rug

Old chair + sample paint pot + fabric offcut = new chair!

Households in the UK generated three million tonnes of wood waste in 2016. The majority of this waste ends up in landfill.

Copper pipes to candlesticks or plant holders

Mirror frames to picture frames

Lab stools to plant stands

The Eco-Thrifty Furniture Checklist

Look around second-hand furniture stores, online auction sites, flea markets and car boot fairs and see if there's something that fits the bill. You can often find high-value items with little wear for a fraction of the retail price if you're prepared to rummage.

If you're buying a piece to replace something that is a bit tired or damaged, consider having it restored, repaired or recovered first.

If it must be new, delve into the sustainability and environmental practices of the companies that you plan to purchase your items from. Look for a Forest Stewardship Council (FSC) label.

Avoid all furniture made from tropical hardwood or other non-sustainable sources, unless it's second-hand. Opt for solid wood furniture from Western countries with strict sustainability guidelines.

Many of the materials used in mass-produced furniture have potentially harmful components. Furniture comprised of chipboard or MDF (medium density fibreboard) sometimes contains formaldehyde, which is carcinogenic and toxic to the environment. The formaldehyde used in the construction of particle-board furniture leaks from the product for up to ten years after it's made – this is known as "outgassing", which has been linked to some cancers.

Modern fabrics can also contain chemicals, especially PVC and polyurethane, which contain formaldehyde, acetone and other nasties.

Consider items made from reclaimed wood – wood that had a previous use, such as for floorboards or rafters. Or if you're handy with a hammer, try some of the reclaimed furniture makes in this section!

Buy furniture that will last. It may cost more but see it as a lifetime's investment, and a way to play your part in creating a sustainable future.

Cheap, mass-produced furniture is designed to be thrown away after a few years, whereas a good-quality piece of furniture can last several lifetimes.

Pallets

Pallet furniture is all the rage. Pallets, mostly made from pine or oak, are often found ditched beside shops or in skips, ready to go to landfill. But these humble yet versatile wooden products have so much more life left in them. They can be made into all manner of items of furniture, from a wine rack and shoe storage to a three-piece suite.

Here's a stylish coffee table on castors, which can be made in a day!

Simply by adding a glass top and painting the pallets, you are elevating your humble pallet table into something magnificent and ever so chic!

PALLET COFFEE TABLE

Method

First, procure your pallets, but be sure to ask before you take them away. Ideally try to get hold of four or five to give you more options in terms of size and finish.

Begin by stacking them to decide what looks best – you will find that every pallet has its own unique characteristics and oddities so this part of the process can take a little time.

When you have your configuration, you will need to spend time preparing the pallets by first fixing any areas that have split or are loose with wood glue and nails, then use sandpaper to smooth the surfaces and prepare them for stain or wax polish.

Attach the pallets together with wood screws. If using extra wood for the top of the table for a less rustic finish, cut to size, lightly sand and attach with wood screws.

Apply the wood stain as per the instructions on the container.

Attach the castor wheels to the base of the table, one on each corner, but make sure they line up.

Your table is complete! For an extra-special finish, you can add a glass top which can be cut to size by a picture framers or DIY store.

Materials

2 or 3 large packing pallets

5 cm x 10 cm (2 in. x 4 in.) wood planks cut to size for the top (optional)

Wood glue

Wood saw

Wood stain or wax polish

Nails and wood screws

Sandpaper

4 swivel-plate castor wheels

SWING SHELF

Materials

Piece of wood for shelf or shelves (aim for a width of 20 to 25 cm (7.9 in. to 9.8 in.); the length is your choice)

Strong sisal rope (or similar)

Wood glue

Copper pressure cups (very cheap and available from ironmongers)

Hook

Equipment

Wood saw

Sandpaper

Drill and drill bits

Masking tape

Method

For your wood a floorboard or scaffolding board will do – these boards can be picked up cheaply from a reclamation yard. The more rustic the better!

Prepare your shelf by cutting the wood to size. Most DIY stores will cut your wood to size if you're purchasing it from them; alternatively, get a tape measure and pencil and draw a line to ensure a neat line when sawing.

Sand the edges so they're smooth, then drill four holes – two sets on each side – as per the diagram below. Then sand the edges of the holes.

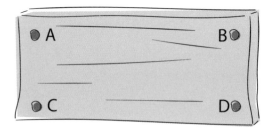

Next, cut your rope to size. First, position your wood at the height you want it on your wall then measure the distance from the shelf to the ceiling. Double that measurement and cut two pieces of rope to that length.

Fix a piece of masking tape around one end of one length of rope and thread it down through the top of hole A, making

sure there is enough rope to tie a secure knot underneath the shelf (we will call this the "beneath knot"). Tie another knot above the shelf, as close to the hole as you can (we will call this the "above knot").

Then fix a piece of masking tape around the opposite end of the same piece of rope. This time, tie the "above knot" first, then thread the remainder through hole B, making sure you leave enough rope underneath to tie the "beneath knot".

Repeat the process for holes C and D with your second piece of rope, making sure the rope lengths are equal at each section to the first piece of rope – this is very important!

Then finish by removing the masking tape and gluing the copper cups to the loose ends of the rope to ensure a professional finish.

Hang securely with a hook screwed into the ceiling and arrange some favourite finds on it.

MAKE A PHOTO FRAME FROM THIS BOOK!

Being eco-conscious on a budget doesn't mean living somewhere without creature comforts and a few knick-knacks. Without going all Marie Kondo about it, we all have items that give us enormous pleasure – happy memories distilled into objects – and these precious items should have pride of place in your home. Here's a lovely way to display your favourite photos rather than storing them on your phone! The wonderful thing about this make is that the book remains intact, but you end up with a rather special and unique self-standing picture frame.

Materials

A favourite photo

This book! (Or another to practise on)

Pencil

Metal ruler

Stanley knife with sharp blade

Cutting mat

Fine sandpaper (optional)

Clear document wallet or photo protector

Scissors

Acid-free masking tape

Method

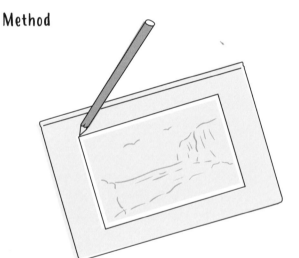

Choose a photo and hold it against the cover of the book to make sure there is plenty of space for a border. Draw a square or rectangle that is slightly smaller than your image.

Next, cut out the shape you have drawn. You will need to place the front cover flat onto a piece of board or a cutting mat and use a sharp Stanley knife and metal ruler for a clean edge. Tip: use double-sided tape on the underside of the metal ruler so it doesn't slip.

Clean up the edges, if necessary, with fine sandpaper.

Cut down a clear document wallet or photo protector to keep your image clean and dust-free, slot your image inside and stick the wallet into place with acid-free masking tape on the reverse of the cover.

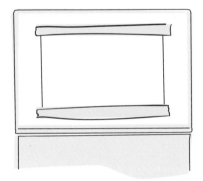

Once you've completed one, you will want to make more! Start collecting old hardback books from charity shops and car boots and you'll have a unique and beautiful collection of picture frames.

T-SHIRT QUILT

This is a wonderful way to preserve your favourite T-shirts after they have passed their wear-by date. T-shirt fabric is the softest and cosiest and is perfect for snuggling. It makes a quilt of approximately 135 x 200 cm (53 x 78 in.).

Materials

10 T-shirts for a full-size quilt (using the front and back of each T-shirt), which will fit a single bed

Iron and ironing board

Cotton

Scissors

Sewing machine (or needle, thread and extreme patience!)

Tape measure

30 x 30 cm (11.8 x 11.8 in.) piece of cardboard for your patchwork template

Pins

Iron-on interfacing

Fabric for the backing of your quilt – use an old single sheet if you have one

Fire-retardant quilt batting (the soft stuff that acts as the filling in the sandwich between the front and the back of the quilt) – the eco-friendliest is made from bamboo. All are readily available from craft stores or online

Bias binding for the edge of the quilt

Give your T-shirts an iron and then cut each along the edge, and remove the neck and cuffs so that you have two large pieces of fabric from each T-shirt.

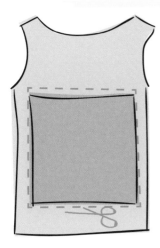

Cut the squares from your T-shirts, using your patchwork template as a guide. If there are patterns or words on the T-shirts, take a bit of time to work out which part of the design you want on show. Cut interfacing to the same size as the template and then iron on the interfacing to each T-shirt square – this is not essential but it does make the fabric easier to sew as stretchy material can be difficult to work with.

When all the pieces have been cut out, lay them out on a clean floor to determine where each piece will go – see which designs and colours work best together. For this pattern we are working on the premise of five rows of four squares.

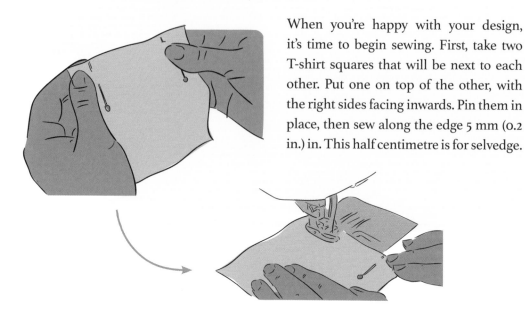

When you're happy with your design, it's time to begin sewing. First, take two T-shirt squares that will be next to each other. Put one on top of the other, with the right sides facing inwards. Pin them in place, then sew along the edge 5 mm (0.2 in.) in. This half centimetre is for selvedge.

Continue sewing the squares together in this way. For ease, sew separate rows together first, and then sew the rows together to form the quilt (rather than making the whole quilt straight away).

When the T-shirt pieces are all sewn together, give it an iron and turn over to tie up loose threads. Measure it to check how short or oversized it is compared to the average single quilt, which is approximately 135 x 200 cm (53 x 78 in.). Remember, you can make it any size you wish!

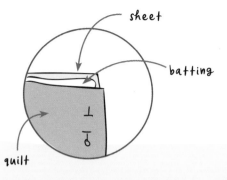

Cut the batting and old sheet to approximately 135 x 200 cm (53 x 78 in.) and pin everything together (right sides facing out) – sheet on the bottom, batting in the middle and quilt on top. Sew pieces together. For a more "quilty" effect, sew along the lines of the edges of each T-shirt square.

Remember to tie loose ends and trim edges for your sewing as you go along to avoid getting threads in a tangle.

Next you will need some bias binding which will cover the raw edges and give your quilt a professional finish. Look online for ways to make your own bias binding out of oddments of fabric, or purchase some from haberdashers or craft stores.

Begin by cutting four lengths of bias binding that are slightly longer than your quilt edges – make sure you have 2.5 cm (1 in.) excess bias at each edge. Then unfold the bias binding and pin the right side of the binding against the front of your quilt, aligning the edge against the raw edge of the quilt. Pin into place.

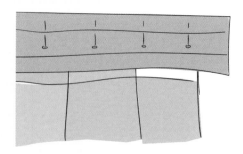

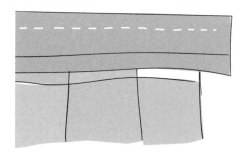

Now sew along the first crease, making sure to catch the front and back of the quilt.

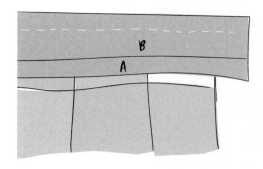

Next, fold up flap A. Then fold flap B up so it's flat against the quilt, and turn the whole thing over so the back of the quilt is facing you.

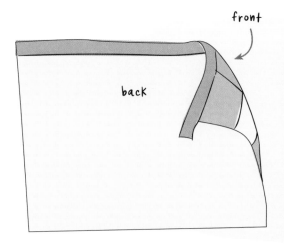

Fold the binding over to the back of the quilt so you have equal widths of bias on the front and back, then iron for a neat crease. Turn the quilt over again and pin the front and back of the binding into place. Sew a running stitch a couple of millimetres from the edge of the binding for a neat finish with the top of the quilt facing you.

There are a couple of options for finishing bias binding edges. If you're feeling adventurous, look online for tutorials on making mitred corners. However, the simplest way is to square off the ends and tuck in a small amount to avoid fraying. To do this, make sure the back of the quilt is facing you. Take one end of binding and fold up section A. Then fold section B so the binding is flat against the back of the quilt and pin in place. Turn the quilt over and sew running stitch a couple of millimetres from the edge of the binding for a neat finish. Repeat for all the loose ends of binding.

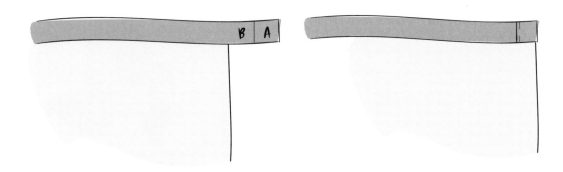

Quick Eco-Thrifty DIY Tips

A piece of oilcloth can be tightly secured with a rubber band to keep a brush (or roller) moist for a day or two in between painting sessions.

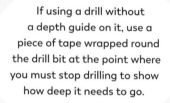

If using a drill without a depth guide on it, use a piece of tape wrapped round the drill bit at the point where you must stop drilling to show how deep it needs to go.

When painting ceilings and walls, tie the roller to a pole. It gives an even pressure and a whole room can be painted with very little effort.

Decant paint into a small bowl when painting with a paintbrush, as this will keep the can free of the impurities (dust, wood particles, etc.) that your brush may pick up as you work.

When drilling into walls (especially brick) a lot of dust will come out and make a mess. So fold a large sticky note into a V-shape and stick it directly under the place to be drilled. The dust falls into the sticky note.

Paintbrushes that have dried hard can be rejuvenated – after a spell in hot vinegar, comb the bristles with a fork and keep in shape with an elastic band until dry.

On first opening a new tin of paint, tie a piece of string tightly between the two rivets where the handle connects. This provides a place to wipe the brush and rest it without getting paint all over the tin.

To rejuvenate masking tape, put the tape in a microwave oven with a glass of water. Set the oven on full for about a minute. Switch off and check the tape has become quite warm but hasn't overheated. The tape will now peel off just as it did when new.

To prevent tools becoming rusty in the toolbox, pop in some silica packets (make use of the little white packets found in lots of packaging) – as they help absorb damp.

Sugar soap used for preparing walls and furniture before painting is also good for removing gloss paint splashes from doors and window ledges. It just comes off with a rub and a cloth.

After using gloss paint for a while, it starts to go thick and is harder to paint with. Add a generous squirt of homemade washing-up liquid (see page 20) to the paint. Give it a good stir and it will go further, spread better and will not leave brush marks.

To paint railings, use a car-cleaning mitten. Put paint on the mitten, take off the surplus and then grip the railing with the mitt and run your hand up and down. It's easy, quick and much less tedious than using a brush. Keep the mitten for when you are next doing "dirty jobs" like clearing guttering.

When painting pipes which are fixed to a wall, cut out a piece of cardboard, place this behind the pipes to be painted and then paint in the usual way. This will prevent any paint getting onto the wall behind.

When using a ladder against painted masonry, put old socks over the ends of the ladder to prevent it damaging the stonework.

To paint a wall with emulsion but with no brush or roller, a sponge can be used instead.

When peeling paper off a ceiling, first put an old sheet over the back of the stepladder, tying the two adjacent ends to create a bag into which the paper can be placed as soon as it is removed. This saves a lot of cleaning up at the end of the day.

Cat litter can be used for absorbing oil spills in garages etc. Dilute any spills with paint thinner or white spirit, sprinkle with cat litter and sweep up when the liquid has been absorbed.

If sash windows are stiff to open and shut, put candle wax or soap down the side runners.

If you have wallpaper left over after a decorating project, use as linings for drawers or as wrapping paper.

IN THE GARDEN
The All-Natural Eco-Thrifty Garden

If you are lucky enough to have your own patch of nature it's a place where you can make a positive difference to our environmental impact and support the local wildlife at the same time. Sustainable gardening can be many things, from growing your own produce to reduce your carbon footprint in terms of the consumables that you purchase, to collecting rainwater in butts or using grey water on your plants instead of using hoses and sprinklers, and being mindful of the composition of the products that you use to maintain your garden.

Unusual Planters

Get creative with your old bits and bobs that might otherwise have ended up in landfill. Any vessel can be adapted into a decorative planter – just check out these ideas!

Create a garden masterpiece with a vintage typewriter

An old pair of boots makes a cosy home for spring flowers

Repurposed tyres make robust planters for fruits and vegetables

Create hanging baskets with helmets or even flippers — the sky is the limit

Grow Your Own – on a Small or Grand Scale

Growing your own is very much in fashion once more – and for many reasons. It's economical and ensures that all your produce is organic and pesticide-free. It also reduces your carbon footprint in terms of the amount of purchased consumables and the subsequent food waste you create.

The physical benefits of gardening are also worth considering: working away in the garden can be as challenging as any aerobics class, and the exertion releases endorphins, which alleviate stress and lower blood pressure.

If you live in an apartment with no outside space that needn't stop you. A window box or pots on a windowsill can be enough to grow a range of fresh fruit, vegetables and herbs, saving you a fair few pounds on your grocery bill, especially if you're always buying bags of salad and herbs – think of how much you spend on salad throughout the year! Allotments and community gardening initiatives are another way to develop your green fingers and grow your own produce. Salad leaves and herbs can also be grown in the kitchen, ensuring fresh leaves all year round.

Replacing just 20 per cent of the food you eat with produce from a homegrown source could reduce your carbon footprint by nearly 32 kg (70 lb) of CO_2 per year.

No More Plastic Pots

Empty toilet-roll tubes make ideal containers for growing crops from seeds. If growing fruit, try growing the smaller-sized varieties indoors as they are more likely to ripen.

Fold in one end of the toilet roll to create a spill-proof container. Fill the container halfway with compost and moisten with water, then add a little starting mix before placing a seed in each container. Add a covering of potting soil to cover the seeds and then moisten with water. Find a suitable flat-based waterproof container to house your toilet-roll planters so that the water doesn't soak through onto your windowsill or floor. A sunny spot will help the seedlings to sprout.

If you have space in a garden, you can plant the whole plant – including the container – into the ground (or in larger pots outdoors). The cardboard will protect the roots from pests before it biodegrades.

Keep an eye on the moisture level of your plants and within as little as four weeks you could have your first crop of lettuces! Trim the outer leaves with kitchen scissors and it's ready to eat.

Plants to grow in your toilet-roll pots:

Gem lettuce

Cherry tomatoes

Raspberries

Dill

Parsley

Blackcurrants and redcurrants

Sage

Rocket

HERB JARS

These jars are not only decorative but they're a neat way of growing your own herbs on a windowsill for use in cooking or making herbal teas (see page 60).

You will need

Seeds to grow herb plants, such as parsley, thyme, basil, oregano, coriander, rosemary, mint or chives (you can purchase these from supermarkets or garden centres)

A selection of jam jars

Gravel, grit or small stones

Compost

Soil to cover stones

Water

Instructions

Clean your jam jars with washing-up liquid and warm water, then rinse and leave to dry.

Fill the base of your jars with gravel, grit or small stones – make sure it's a minimum of 5 cm (2 in.) in depth. These stones are vital as they will draw the water and prevent mould forming on your plants.

Fill the jars about two thirds full with compost. Plant three herb seeds in each jar.

Once shoots start to form, add more soil around the base of each plant. Then water your plants and they're ready to be placed on a windowsill – although if your chosen herb doesn't thrive in direct sunlight, find a shadier spot.

Be sure to trim them regularly to avoid them getting "leggy".

Now you can enjoy herbs all year round, and they're easy to grab when you're preparing meals.

MAKE YOUR OWN HERBAL TEABAGS

Making your own herbal teas will reduce both your caffeine intake and your expenditure! It's also fun mixing different herbs to create your own blends. Natural cotton drawstring teabags are simple to make and you can make a batch to store in a tin or Mason jar – they not only look beautiful but are reusable too.

Makes approx. 50 teabags

You will need

1 m² unbleached muslin

Scissors

Unbleached embroidery thread or similar (for the drawstring)

Sewing machine (or needle and thimble)

Cotton

Your fresh or dried herbs (and spices – optional)

Instructions

Create a template or use a ruler and mark out 6.5 x 7.5 cm (2.55 x 2.95 in.) oblongs on the muslin – the reason why they aren't square is to allow for the drawstring opening at the top of the bag.

When you have your cut pieces, take one piece and fold over and pin 1.5 cm (0.6 in.) at the top of the longer length to create the tunnel for the drawstring. Sew this fold in place and repeat on another fabric piece (you can use a sewing machine or hand stitch the fabric using a running stitch).

Pin these two pieces together with the raw edges facing out and carefully sew the two sides below the drawstring tunnel. Then sew along the bottom to create the bag.

Trim away some of the raw edges but be careful not to cut into the stitches.

Turn the bag right side out, so that the raw edges are on the inside of the bag.

Cut an 18 cm (7 in.) length of your cotton. Use a needle to guide this thread through the tunnel at the top of the bag. Make sure that you leave a short length at both ends for the drawstring to work effectively.

Repeat until you have used up your fabric!

- Get creative with your herb mixes. You can buy dried herbs cheaply in bulk from health food stores. Use a teaspoon each of different herbs and spices and let your taste buds and imagination run wild. Add in your fresh or dried herbs and spices – fill the bag so it's bulging!

- Your homemade teabags can be stored until needed – the fresh herbs will keep their potency even when they have dried.

- Boil some water, pick out your favourite cup, drop in a bag and pour over boiled water. Leave to infuse for a few minutes, then drink and enjoy!

To reuse your cotton teabags, clean out the used tea, then give them a rinse in water (without detergent) and leave to air-dry. If this all sounds a bit fiddly, you can purchase pre-made bags online relatively cheaply.

MAKE YOUR OWN ECO-FRIENDLY BUG SPRAY

It goes without saying that it's best to avoid any products with irritant or toxic substances in your garden as they can harm you, your family, pets and local wildlife. Repellents and sprays also produce a large amount of greenhouse gases during the factory process. Here is a simple eco-friendly spray to deter the not-so friendly bugs from your garden, like blackfly and aphids, which will munch through your flowers and crops given half the chance.

Ingredients

2 handfuls fresh
   mint leaves

4 garlic cloves

2 tbsp vinegar

1 l (1.75 pt) water

Spray bottle

Method

Begin by blending the mint leaves and garlic cloves in a pestle and mortar or a food processor.

Combine all of the ingredients in a saucepan and bring to the boil.

Allow to cool and leave to steep for four hours.

Strain the solution into your spray bottle and it's ready to use. Simply squirt the liquid directly onto affected plants and watch the results.

Composting

This is an excellent way to do your bit to reduce the amount of food and garden waste that goes to landfill – it's believed that around 30 per cent of waste sent to landfill could be composted instead – and the added bonus is that you end up with good-quality compost for the garden without any extra financial outlay.

An Eco-Thrifty Compost Bin

This is one of the simplest and most useful constructions for the garden. Simply stand four pallets up on their sides with the pallet slats facing inward to form a container.

Bind the pallets together firmly with garden wire or cable ties. It doesn't need to be perfect as the more air that reaches the compost the better it will be.

Tips for Composting

Designate an area of the garden for a heap, which must be a minimum of a cubic metre. Be aware that the items you place on the heap may attract wildlife, so make sure it is a good distance from your house and away from where children might want to play. It also needs to be in an area with good drainage and in a partially sunny and partially shaded spot.

Prepare a layer of twigs and branches at the bottom of the heap to provide vertical airflow through the material; on top of this, mix in your browns and greens (see page 69) with thin layers of dead flowers, manure and straw. Sheep manure is probably the richest source of nutrients, just ahead of horse manure. Chances are you can probably find both for free if you know a farmer or horse owner.

If you want your compost heap to remain active during winter, be sure to keep it in a place that gets lots of sunlight so that the compost can form quickly. Alternatively, insulate the sides with hay to keep the compost warm.

Turn your compost pile every two weeks for fast results. The finished compost should look and smell like rich, dark soil and have a crumbly rather than sticky texture. Compost can be made in six to eight weeks, or it can take a year or more. The more effort you put in, the quicker you get results. Your compost pile should be moist all the way through so be sure to wet each new layer every time you add one. Do not leave a finished compost pile standing unprotected as it will lose nutrients. Special breathable compost cover sheets can be found at any garden centre.

Don't add the following items to your compost pile: charcoal or coal ashes, which contain high amounts of sulphur; cat or dog droppings, which might contain disease; or weeds, which will only grow again once you spread your compost. And unless you fancy attracting rats to your garden, avoid adding eggs or meat to the mix.

Weed-free and pesticide-free grass clippings bring nitrogen to your compost – so be sure to mix them in well with the browns to avoid smells, prevent a slimy texture and get the maximum benefit from the grass. Let the worms get to work!

Browns and greens refer to the different items that you can compost. Green items are fresh, moist items – not necessarily green! – such as grass clippings and vegetable peelings, whereas brown items are dry, older items, such as dead leaves, wood shavings and pieces of cardboard. The green items are nitrogen-rich, whereas the brown items are carbon-rich, and the most successful compost heaps contain a balance of the two.

Plant Trees

Offset your carbon emissions and boost the oxygen levels in your garden simply by planting trees. Grow trees that are native to your local climate as these will grow more quickly. Trees with broad leaves, such as oak, elm and horse chestnut, are the most efficient at absorbing carbon and enabling photosynthesis. Fruit trees are also great for the garden, providing fresh fruit and encouraging bees and other garden-friendly creatures.

MAKE YOUR OWN TEA-LIGHT HOLDERS FROM RECYCLED TIN CANS

Create something beautiful out of a humble tin can with these
candleholders for summer evenings in the garden.

You will need

Tin cans of varying
sizes (as many as
you can gather)

Scrap paper

Pencil

Scissors

Marker pen

Rubber bands or
paper tape

Towel

Hammer

Nail

Wire or string
for hanging

Soy tea-light candles

Instructions

First give the tin cans a good soak in warm water with your
homemade washing-up liquid (see page 20) to remove the
labels and adhesive, and any remnants of food. Dry thoroughly.

Now consider the design you want to have on the can, whether
it's to be a simple repeating pattern of hearts, for example,
or something elaborate that will encircle the entire sides of
the can. Cut your piece of paper to the size required for your
design and start sketching or trace a design that you like.

When you are happy with your design, use the marker to
create a dotted line on your drawing, with dots around a
centimetre apart.

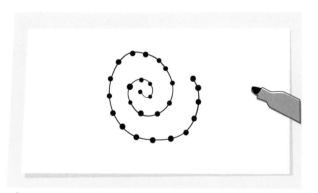

Fill your cans with water and place in the freezer until the water is solid. The reason for this is it will prevent the tin from becoming misshapen when you are making the holes.

Once the water is frozen, attach the piece of paper with your design to the can with rubber bands or paper tape.

Place the can on its side on a towel, preferably outside as it could get messy.

Then use your hammer and nail to make the holes where your dots are placed by positioning the nail over each dot, hammering it into the tin to puncture the metal and then removing the nail. Repeat on the next dot.

When you have finished, make a hole in each side at the top so that you can insert wire or string for a handle.

Allow the ice to melt a little, then pour it out, preferably onto the garden or into a potted plant to avoid waste! Give the can a rinse, being careful not to touch any sharp edges on the inside around the holes.

Use your string or wire to create a handle so you can hang the lantern on a tree branch or hook.

Insert your candle and it's ready to use.

MAKE A BUG HOTEL

Attract solitary bees and other insects into the garden with this simple bug hotel. This is a great way to repurpose items that you're likely to have to hand.

You will need

A large, empty food can

Can opener

Nail

Hammer

String

Bamboo canes – these must be hollow and can be of varying sizes

Secateurs

Instructions

Use a can opener to remove the bottom from an empty, clean can, leaving the centre tube. Place the base in the recycling. Make two small holes with your nail and hammer (big enough to thread string through) about halfway down the tin and about 5 cm (2 in.) apart.

Carefully push one end of the string into each of the holes and pull a small section through. Then knot each end and pull out the string so you have the means for hanging up your bug hotel.

Take a piece of bamboo and cut it with the secateurs into equal lengths that are a few centimetres longer than the can. Take another piece of bamboo and do the same again until you have enough canes so that when they are slotted into the can they are packed together tightly and don't move.

When it is finished, hang up your bug hotel so the can is on its side and the bamboo lies horizontally in the can. Be careful to pick a spot that gets some sunshine in the day but is sheltered from wind.

Quick Eco-Thrifty Garden Tips

Good-quality second-hand gardening equipment can be picked up very cheaply – and sometimes even for free. Before you buy anything new, look on the Freecycle website, where you should be able to find a dedicated Freecycle community in your area. All the items are free!

Cut up old stockings and tights into strips to make plant ties – the soft, flexible nature of the fabric will protect new shoots as they grow bigger.

An old potato peeler does an excellent job of removing weeds from the lawn.

Car boot sales and recycling centres are also great places to pick up gardening equipment at bargain prices.

Make a garden kneeler by filling an old hot-water bottle with polystyrene chips. It's wipe cleanable and will make those long hours in the garden a little more comfortable.

Don't spend money on buying supporting canes; instead collect twigs. They look far less conspicuous and they're free!

Collect fallen leaves when they are wet, then store in bin bags for two years. The result is a nutritious leaf mulch which can be used to cover your most prized plants.

Shop around for cheap seeds, such as in end-of-season sales and even on eBay.

Waste water from washing-up is perfect for watering gardens. Bathwater can also be used to water the garden but it's best not to use it on edible crops.

Old banana skins are rich in potassium and will do wonders for rose bushes when buried deep into the soil beside them.

A past-repair garden hose can be cut into pieces to resemble snakes. Paint stripes on them and distribute round a vegetable plot to deter rodents and birds.

Butterflies are repelled by the smell of tomato plants, so plant these among your leeks to prevent them from laying eggs that will turn into caterpillars that could eat your crop.

A humane method of sending moles packing is to plant glass bottles (without lids on) into the unsightly molehills with the tops of the bottles showing, so that the noise of the wind travels through their tunnels, encouraging them to move to a more peaceful location.

IN THE BATHROOM
Eco-Natural Beauty

Essential body care can generate a lot of waste as many beauty, skincare and hygiene products are often packaged in non-recyclable containers and boxed in cardboard and plastic – not to mention the additional laminated sheets of instructions, applicators and even plastics in the products themselves.

It's what is contained in your beauty products that also requires careful scrutiny. Companies are not required by law to list all the ingredients, so in most cases there is no way of knowing the amount of synthetic man-made ingredients that have been added – many products have been found to contain microplastics, phthalates and parabens. According to the Campaign for Safe Cosmetics (CSC), legal loopholes enable the cosmetics companies to use these chemicals without testing for damage to health. Subsequent testing has found that phthalates and parabens can damage internal organs after prolonged external use. Not only this but many cosmetics reach the sea, where the microplastics spread into the food chain.

But there is a way to be eco-thrifty and keep up your beauty routine. Be mindful when shopping for beauty products – the companies that are truly eco-friendly and human-friendly (!) will list all ingredients. Look for the ones that use only natural or naturally derived ingredients. These products often cost more than average – and it's a shame that sustainable and eco-friendly goods tend to come at a premium – so this chapter contains some beauty products that can be made cheaply and simply in your kitchen.

SHAMPOO BARS

Shampoo in a bar! These luxurious bars are brilliant for reducing your plastic consumption and saving money. They are simple to make too – make up a batch for yourself and your friends. They're also highly portable – if you're going on holiday, you won't find a puddle of gunge at the bottom of your bag as there is nothing to spill and they can be taken on board aircraft in your hand luggage.

Makes two standard-sized shampoo bars

Ingredients

125 g Castile melt and pour soap base (available at chemists and online)

1½ tsp argan oil

½ tsp black treacle

10 drops lavender essential oil

10 drops rose essential oil

10 drops jasmine essential oil

Pure alcohol spray

Equipment

Saucepan

Metal or heatproof mixing bowl that fits neatly over your saucepan

Sharp knife

Metal spoon

Dropper

Silicone soap moulds – available from craft suppliers online

Instructions

Begin by cutting your Castile melt and pour soap base into 1 cm (0.4 in.) cubes and placing them in the metal or heatproof bowl.

Fill the saucepan with water so that when you place the metal bowl over the pan the water is just grazing the bowl. Heat the water on a medium heat.

As the contents of the bowl begin to melt, stir the liquid with a metal spoon until it has melted and is a runny consistency – this is your shampoo base.

Once the shampoo base has melted, mix in the argan oil and black treacle.

Remove your shampoo mixture from the heat and allow to cool for five minutes.

Using a dropper, add in the essential oils and mix with the spoon.

Pour the shampoo mixture into your moulds and leave to set overnight.

Once the shampoo is solid, turn it out and slice into palm-sized chunks with a sharp knife.

It's now ready to use and will keep for six months.

Many soap or shampoo bar recipes contain a substance called lye, which can cause breathing difficulties if not handled correctly. This recipe does not contain lye. The essential oils are just a suggestion – choose your own favourite aromas!

NATURAL DEODORANT

We spend a lot of money on having nice-smelling armpits; according to statistics, the global antiperspirant and deodorant market for 2018 was worth an estimated $72.7 billion, and when you consider that the majority of these products are packaged in single-use plastic and cans, that's a scary amount of waste added to landfill each year. Make a difference by making your own deodorant, and sharing the recipe with your friends.

Ingredients

8 g milk of magnesia or magnesium hydroxide (available from chemists or online)

60 g distilled water

60 g witch hazel

20 g arrowroot powder

30 g aloe vera gel

30 g bicarbonate of soda

15 drops of peppermint essential oil

1 roll-on bottle

Instructions

Mix the milk of magnesia and the distilled water into a bowl and place to one side.

Mix the witch hazel, arrowroot powder, aloe vera gel, bicarbonate of soda and essential oil into a separate container, making sure the powdered ingredients leave no lumps.

Pour the milk of magnesia and distilled water mixture into the other mixture and stir well.

Pour into a roll-on bottle (you could recycle old bought deodorants for this purpose) and secure the top.

Shake well before use. This will keep for six months.

SOLID PERFUME

This is more of a nice-to-have than a must-have, but being eco-thrifty means you can have a few luxuries. It's also a fraction of the price of shop-bought perfumes and completely unique! It makes a lovely eco-luxe gift too.

Ingredients

30 g beeswax pellets

30 g sweet almond essential oil

15 drops of your desired essential oil(s) – it can be a mix of scents (such as rose and vanilla or bergamot and lemon)

Shallow glass screw-top jars to store your perfume (either reuse old ones or buy online)

Instructions

Melt the beeswax and almond oil. This can be done in either a metal or heatproof bowl over a pan of simmering water or in a microwave.

Once melted, carefully drop in your essential oils, mixing them in with a metal teaspoon.

Pour the mixture into the containers and leave to set before screwing on the lid.

The perfume works by applying it with your fingertips. The heat from your fingers liquefies the perfume, which can then be applied to your pulse points.

Experiment with different scents and varying amounts of essential oil to create your own signature scent.

BATH BOMBS

The excitement of watching the fizz of a bath bomb never gets old. Here's the eco-thrifty way to get your fix.

Makes one bomb

Ingredients

60 g bicarbonate of soda

30 g Epsom salts

30 g cornflour

30 g citric acid

3 tsp olive oil (any type is fine)

1 tbsp natural essential oils (you could use a mix of your favourites)

1 tsp natural food colouring

1 tbsp tap water

Bath bomb mould

Instructions

Place all the dry ingredients in a bowl and mix thoroughly with a metal spoon.

Pour the citric acid, olive oil, essential oils, food colouring and water into a jug and mix well.

Slowly pour the wet ingredients into the bowl with the dry ingredients and mix as you go. The mixture should be the consistency of wet sand.

Scoop the mixture into your mould, seal and leave to harden for a couple of hours.

When the bomb has set, it's ready for the bath. Or you can wrap the bath bombs in tissue paper or fabric scraps and keep them or gift them. They'll last for 12 months.

SOAPS

Soap is a lovely gift and once you realize just how easy it is to make, there'll be no stopping you.

Ingredients

500 g of Castile melt and pour soap base*

Coloured liquid soap dye of your choice (optional)

1 tsp of essential oil of your choice (lavender or rose are good options)

100 ml of 90 per cent IPA alcohol

Equipment

Sharp knife

Chopping board

Double-boiler saucepan or a metal bowl (or a heatproof jug and a microwave)

Metal spoon

Soap mould with 500-g capacity

* Melt and pour soap base is available in clear, white or off-white, so it's up to you which one you use.

Instructions

Chop up the melt and pour soap base into 1 cm (0.4 in.) cubes and place into a double boiler or a metal bowl over a saucepan of boiling water or into a heatproof jug to go into the microwave for melting.

Stir the liquid a few times with the metal spoon to make sure there are no lumps, then add a few drops of liquid soap dye (if using) and your essential oil.

Give the mixture a good stir then it's ready to pour into your mould. If using a silicone mould, you will need to place it in a sturdy container – such as a lunchbox, small tin or baking dish – to keep the silicone from warping when you pour in the soap.

Spray a thin layer of the alcohol on top of the soap as this prevents bubbles from forming and will ensure a smooth finish.

Leave the soap to harden for a couple of hours. Remove the silicone mould from the container and, before turning out the soap, give the silicone a gentle squeeze at the base just to make sure it has set properly.

Once set, turn out the soap and cut into blocks with a sharp knife.

Package up in waxed paper or parchment paper to store if not using immediately.

REUSABLE MAKE-UP REMOVER PADS

Cotton-wool pads and make-up remover pads tend by their very nature to be for single use, but here is a simple way to eradicate the need to ever purchase them again by making your own reusable cotton pads. They are very cheap to make, and are kind to both your skin and the environment.

You will need

Flannel or soft cotton fabric (repurposed fabric from an old shirt or other item is ideal)

Fabric scissors

Needle and thread, or a sewing machine and thread

Instructions

Cut out 40 pieces of fabric to the same size – cutting squares is easiest, but you might prefer circles. Aim for a length or diameter of 8 cm (3 in.).

Then, with the wrong side out, place two pieces together and sew three sides, or if sewing circles, leave a gap on the edge of around 5 cm (2 in.) so that you can turn the fabric pocket the right way out.

Over stitch the remaining opening by hand and your fabric pad is complete.

Once used, they can be washed in warm water with a bit of homemade washing-up liquid and hung to dry.

Keep the prettiest ones for your make-up bag and the wonky ones for the dirtiest jobs like removing eye make-up.

And when it comes to removing make-up, instead of applying chemicals to your skin, use coconut oil, which does the job just as well while also being more gentle on your skin.

Quick Eco-Thrifty Beauty Tips

Use bars of soap rather than liquid soap that comes in plastic dispensers.

Buy or make your own shampoo, conditioner and shower-gel bars, rather than relying on plastic-packaged liquid alternatives.

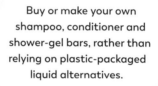

Wash your hair less. Most shampoos contain parabens, sulphates and other chemicals which enter the water system through our drains. Human hair is perfectly capable of regulating its own cleanliness without the use of shampoos and conditioners. You could try rinsing it with apple cider vinegar, which rebalances the natural oils in the hair, or, to reduce your environmental impact, simply opt to wash it only once a week.

Avoid aerosol deodorants, which release VOCs and other toxic chemicals into the environment, and use rock salt or stick deodorants instead.

For women, the use of a menstrual cup negates the need for disposable sanitary products.

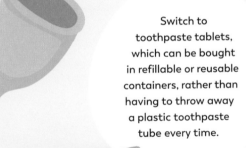

Switch to toothpaste tablets, which can be bought in refillable or reusable containers, rather than having to throw away a plastic toothpaste tube every time.

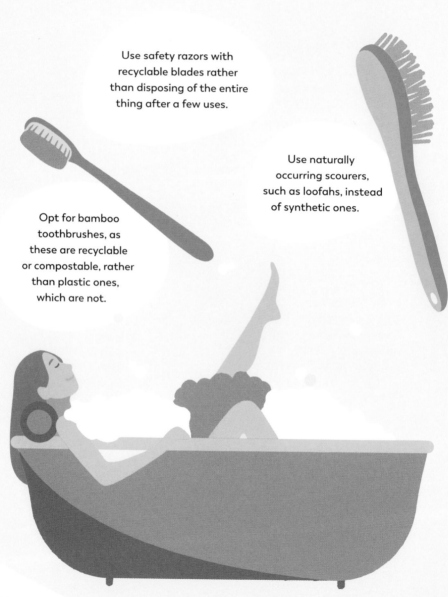

Use safety razors with recyclable blades rather than disposing of the entire thing after a few uses.

Use naturally occurring scourers, such as loofahs, instead of synthetic ones.

Opt for bamboo toothbrushes, as these are recyclable or compostable, rather than plastic ones, which are not.

Buy a single large tub of coconut oil for moisturizing, wiping away make-up, conditioning your hair and for use in homemade scrubs rather than buying individually packaged items for each application.

If you must use cotton buds, opt for ones made of paper, not plastic.

Toilet paper is something we simply can't do without! But recycled and eco-friendly versions are available.

Eco-Thrifty Beauty Challenge

See how many of your regular beauty products can be homemade or refilled.

Bamboo toothbrush

Natural body brushes

Homemade solid perfume

Reusable cotton wipes

Refillable soap dispenser

Epsom salts

Homemade shampoo bar

Natural loofah

Pumice for
hard skin

Paper earbuds

IN THE KITCHEN
Nutritious and Natural

The kitchen is the heart of the home but it is also the place that generates the most waste! Food waste in particular is a big issue: the UK alone bins 7 million tonnes of food each year; the amount of money wasted per household is around £500 per year; and between 30 and 40 per cent of all food is wasted in the US. This chapter offers eco-thrifty ways to make your food go further, from pickling and fermenting to batch cooking and making delicious meals with your leftovers.

Top Tips to Reduce Food Waste

Here are some sobering statistics from Friends of the Earth:

- One third of food produced globally is wasted or lost.

- One truckful of plastic is dumped in the sea every minute – and it is believed that by 2050 there will be a greater density of plastic than fish in the world's oceans.

- One billion black plastic food trays end up in landfill in the UK each year, with this statistic rising.

- 50 million chickens are wasted in the UK every year.

Here are some easy fixes to help you reduce food waste in your home:

Store food properly – use airtight containers and keep the fridge tidy so you know what you've got and how long the items will last.

Be sure to buy products that will remain in date for when you plan to cook them. Don't be taken in by offers where you end up buying more food than necessary.

Plan your meals for the week and be aware of the amount of food you are purchasing – it might seem tedious, but planning for the week and only buying what you need for all of your meals will avoid waste. Include big dishes in your meal plan, such as curries or stew, which can be eaten over a few days, reducing the need to cook every day.

Make the most of leftovers, e.g. use a roast chicken carcass for stock or a delicious soup.

You can freeze more types of food than you might expect, including meat, fish, eggs, milk, cheese, bread, and fruit and veg (although these might go squishy when defrosted, they will still be good to eat). Sliced bread will last for months in the freezer, and you will only need to take out the slices you want to eat then use the "defrost" setting of your toaster. Check online to see how long certain foods can be frozen for.

Do a tally of all the food and drink items that you throw away over a month. You're likely to see a pattern forming where the same items are ending up in the bin, such as salads, bread, meals that you buy in offers that seem good value but you don't really want to eat, certain fruit that has become overripe, the same things that get discarded in lunchboxes... If you don't like something, don't buy it in the first place!

Eat first before you shop. If you're hungry, you're likely to buy more than you need, and you'll be more inclined to buy sugary snacks.

Remember that some items don't need to be thrown away when they're slightly past their prime.

Cooked food is not usually suitable for your home compost, so a waste-free household should deal with leftovers the old-fashioned way: eat them! One of the easiest and most cost-effective things to do with your dinner leftovers is to pack them up and have them for lunch the next day. Wet leftovers can go in bamboo containers or multi-use lunchboxes, while dry leftovers can be wrapped in beeswax wraps or paper bags. Large quantities of leftovers can be chilled and then frozen to be eaten as a quick and easy meal at a later date.

We don't need a handful of people doing zero waste perfectly. We need millions of people doing it imperfectly.

Anne-Marie Bonneau

Fun Ways to Extend the Life of Your Fruit and Veg

We're spoiled for choice when it comes to food and expect to only eat items when they're at their best and ripest, but some items don't need to be ditched if they're past their prime. Fruit that's gone a bit soft might not seem as appealing to eat but it can make the ideal ingredient for smoothies, jams and chutneys. Here are some tips on what to do with an abundance of fruit or vegetables:

Pears and apples should be wrapped individually in newspaper and stored in wooden boxes or drawers in a cool, dark place – an unheated garage or shed is ideal. Check on the fruits regularly for ones that have gone off.

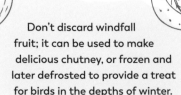

Don't discard windfall fruit; it can be used to make delicious chutney, or frozen and later defrosted to provide a treat for birds in the depths of winter.

All fruits can be dried, but only use blemish-free fruits for this. Wash, pit and slice the fruits, then blanch them by steaming for five minutes then plunging the pieces into cold water. Dip them in a mixture of water and lemon juice to reduce browning and leave them to dry on a kitchen towel. Once completely dry, place on parchment-lined baking trays and place them in the oven on a low heat for four hours. Let them stand overnight and then freeze them in airtight containers until required.

If you have the shed or garage space, pick up an old chest of drawers from a junk shop and use it to store your root vegetables. Spread a layer of sand at the bottom of each drawer and place a layer of vegetables on top. Then cover the vegetables with sand and add more vegetables on top until you reach the top of the drawer. Label and date the drawers.

Strawberries, raspberries, currants and hedgerow fruits can be frozen. Open-freeze the fruits by spreading them on trays and placing directly in the freezer. Once frozen, decant them into airtight containers. This stops them from sticking to each other.

Potatoes can be scrubbed and stored in hessian sacks in a cool, dry place.

If you have food that you know you're not going to eat but it's still fit for human consumption, pop it on the OLIO app (www.olioex.com) – an initiative where people who live nearby can come and pick up your unwanted food so it's not wasted.

FERMENTING – MAKE YOUR OWN KIMCHI

Fermented food is good for gut health and is an eco-thrifty way to use up leftover vegetables. Kimchi is a combination of fermented vegetables and salt. It's rich in probiotics and vitamins A, B and C, and is a staple served in many South Korean households.

Ingredients

1 medium napa cabbage (also known as Chinese cabbage), chopped into 1 cm (0.4 in.) cubes

Water

1 carrot, grated

1 tbsp table salt

1 tbsp caster sugar

1 tbsp chilli flakes

1 garlic clove, minced

1 thumbnail-sized piece fresh root ginger, minced

4 spring onions, sliced

5 radishes, sliced

Instructions

Place the cabbage in a bowl with the salt, cover with water, then pop a plate on top of the cabbage so that it's submerged in the salted water and leave for six hours.

Drain the cabbage but keep the liquid to one side.

Mix the rest of the ingredients in a bowl and add the cabbage.

Decant into a jar, squashing the mixture down so that it's compacted. Pour over the salted water so that it covers the cabbage. Screw on the lid securely.

Leave for five days to ferment, but make sure you remember to open the jar once a day to allow the gas to escape!

Kimchi never goes off; it ripens. But the riper it is, the sourer it becomes, so it's entirely up to your taste buds if it's still edible! It can be used in all manner of dishes to give them a kick. Stir a few tablespoons into stews or soups, or spread onto bread to eat with cheese.

Challenge – Batch Cook All Meals and Snacks for One Week

Batch cooking is when you make more than one portion of food at a time and freeze the rest to be heated up and enjoyed at a later date. It's a great way of making the most of your time, reducing expenditure and planning ahead.

Make protein-rich salads for lunch with lovely leftovers

Make jams and jellies with leftover fruit from the fruit bowl

Popcorn is another great
snack to make in batches
and store in paper bags

Cook up a stew and prepare
vegetables — these can be frozen
and reheated when required

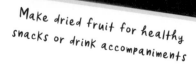

Make a batch of loaves and rolls — freeze the
ones you don't need and slice up the loaves, as
frozen slices can go straight into the toaster

Make dried fruit for healthy
snacks or drink accompaniments

MAKE YOUR OWN BEESWAX WRAPS

The amount of cling film and sandwich bags can really mount up when making packed lunches every day. It's definitely a good thing if you're making your own lunch – shop-bought sandwiches and snacks come with a plethora of packaging that is often thrown into general waste – but you need to stay eco-thrifty when wrapping it up. Beeswax wraps are a magical alternative to cling film. They can be washed and reused, and not only are they environmentally friendly but you'll be making a big saving on single-use plastic. They're easy to make too! Here's how:

Method

Preheat the oven to 95°C (200°F), or use the lowest setting on your oven.

Measure your baking sheet and cut the cotton fabric so it will fit on the baking sheet. Use pinking shears (the scissors that create a zigzag edge) if you have them, as this will prevent your fabric from fraying.

Line your baking sheet with baking paper and place your piece of fabric on top. If you're using a fabric with a pattern, place the pattern face down on the sheet.

Liberally scatter your beeswax pellets all over the fabric. Don't forget those edges!

Place in the oven for around six minutes, or until the pellets have completely melted.

Remove from the oven and use a brush to spread the wax over the fabric so it's evenly coated.

Use tongs or clothes pegs to remove the wrap from the baking tray and hang to dry. You could use a length of string for a makeshift drying rack and peg them up.

Once dry, the wraps are ready to use.

If you prefer bags for your sandwiches, you can fold the wraps in half and sew the two sides together, leaving the top as your opening. Sew on Velcro or a button and buttonhole for a fastening.

You will need

Ruler (optional)

100 per cent cotton fabric

Scissors or pinking shears

Baking paper

Baking sheet

Beeswax pellets

Brush

Tongs

Clothes pegs and string (optional)

Velcro and thread or button and thread for a fastener (optional)

Beeswax wraps are best used on perishable items that you intend to eat within a few hours, like a sandwich or snack. Items such as leftovers or meats are best stored in a reusable plastic or glass container with a lid.

Care for your beeswax wraps by washing them in cool water with washing-up liquid, then hang to dry. When they start to lose their waxiness, you can rejuvenate them by adding more wax pellets.

Buy a Refillable Water Bottle and Coffee Cup

Here's why:

50% of plastic is used only once.

90% of pollution in the ocean is plastic.

The average household incorrectly disposes of around **40 KILOS** (88 lb) of recyclable plastics every year.

It takes

450
YEARS

for some plastics
to biodegrade.

7 MILLION

single-use coffee cups
are thrown away every
day in the UK.*

If you think about it, we never
truly throw anything away – it just
ends up somewhere else.

* Statistics taken from Friends of the Earth.

Challenge – Try to Go One Week Without Plastic

Make your own packed lunches and desk snacks

Buy food from the local market

Take your own fabric bags when shopping to avoid buying plastic bags

For dry ingredients use a refillery

Go foraging

Buy butter wrapped in
paper rather than tubs

Grow your own produce

FRUIT LEATHER

When you have a glut of fruit and you've made all the chutneys, jams and jellies you can handle, what else is there? Fruit leather, of course! These fruity treats are a brilliant way to use up leftover fruit – and they make great, energy-packed snacks.

Ingredients

350 g of the fresh or frozen fruit of your choice – soft fruits work particularly well

4 tbsp local honey

1 tbsp fresh lemon juice

3 tbsp water (judge the amount for yourself as it depends on the liquidity of the fruit)

Method

Start by washing and preparing your fruit, then chop it into bite-size pieces before placing it into a non-stick saucepan with the honey, water and lemon juice. Add the water last as you may only need a dribble.

Cook on a low heat then bring to a simmer and cover for 15 minutes, allowing the fruit to cook down into a pulp.

Take the fruit pulp off the heat and allow to cool.

Once cool, blitz it in a food processor or mash it with a potato masher until smooth. Give it a taste to make sure it's sweet enough for your liking. If not, add in a little more honey or a spoonful of sugar.

Prepare a low-sided baking tray by carefully lining it with baking parchment or a dehydrator sheet. Spread the pulp with a spatula so it's evenly distributed. Place in the oven on its lowest setting for approximately six hours, or do it the old-fashioned way and leave it in the sun to dry out – this can take a little longer, however!

Once the mixture has hardened, leave it to cool before slicing into strips while still attached to the parchment and roll up each strip. If you're eating it straight away, you can do away with the parchment, as seen in the photograph.

The rolls can be stored for a week in the fridge; alternatively, freeze them in an airtight container and keep for up to three months.

Forage for Free Food in the Hedgerows

Foraging is an art, and it can take many years of practice and study to successfully identify all of nature's treasures. Begin by foraging items that are easily identifiable, such as blackberries, wild strawberries and wild garlic. Here are some practical tips to get you ready for foraging:

- Pick your foraging places carefully. Try to avoid areas close to roads as these plants will be contaminated with pollutants; similarly, avoid areas that are likely to have been sprayed with pesticides or sprayed by dogs! Keep to public rights of way unless you have prior permission from the landowner.

- Use a good-quality field guide with images of each hedgerow plant so that you can be sure that you are identifying the plants correctly. If you have any doubts, leave the plant alone as it could be poisonous.

- Be careful not to damage the hedgerows and only pick what you need, leaving plenty for others – and the local wildlife – to enjoy.

- Take a basket or some fabric bags or paper carriers for your picked produce.

- Take secateurs and gloves and wear sensible clothes for traipsing through nettles and undergrowth.

BLACKBERRY VINEGAR

This versatile condiment can be used as a delicious salad dressing and even makes for an effective cold cure! Blackberries are one of the most ubiquitous of the hedgerow plants and are best harvested in August and September.

Ingredients

At least 2 hand-picked punnets (around 500 g) fresh blackberries, washed and with stalks removed

Cider vinegar

Caster sugar

Method

Place your fresh, washed and de-stalked blackberries in a large ceramic or earthenware dish, so that the blackberries cover the base and aren't more than two deep.

Pour over the cider vinegar so that it completely covers the fruit.

Cover the dish with a plate or foil and seal for three days. There is no need to refrigerate during this process.

After the three days, use muslin to strain the mixture into a bowl or jug. This can be a time-consuming process, taking several hours.

Measure the liquid into a large saucepan and for every 0.3 l (half a pint) of liquid, add 225 g (half a pound) of sugar.

Stir the mixture while bringing it to the boil, then simmer for around five minutes or until all the sugar has dissolved.

Take off the heat and allow to cool before decanting the liquid into sterilized bottles with screw tops or pop tops. Label the bottles and store out of sunlight in a dry place. This will keep for a year.

NETTLE BEER

Nettles can be found in abundance from early spring to late autumn. Gathering nettles can be painful if you're not dressed for it – opt for thick gardening gloves and keep your arms and legs covered. Your effort will be rewarded with this distinctive home brew.

Ingredients

1 large fabric grocery bag of nettle tops

5 l (8.8 pt) cold water

Irish moss (available online)

1 thumbnail-sized piece fresh root ginger, minced

500 g caster sugar

11.5 g packet of beer yeast

4 tbsp fresh lemon juice

Method

Give the nettle tops a shake to remove any bugs and rinse under the tap before placing in a large cooking pot with the cold water, Irish moss and ginger. Bring to the boil and simmer for 15 minutes.

Pour in the sugar and stir until dissolved. Once dissolved, take off the heat and allow to cool.

Activate the yeast, using the instructions on the packet, and add this to the mixture along with the lemon juice.

Cover the mixture and leave for three to four days to allow fermentation.

Decant into swing-top or screw-top bottles. Leave to chill in the fridge so it's ready to drink.

Quick Eco-Thrifty Kitchen Tips

Halve a lemon and place inside a fridge to eliminate bad smells. The same principle can be applied to microwaves: place a couple of slices of lemon on a plate and microwave briefly and hey presto!

Add a pinch of salt to 0.5 l (1 pint) of milk to help it stay fresher for longer.

Prevent cheese from going mouldy by storing it with a few lumps of sugar in an airtight container.

Half a lemon placed in a kettle of water and boiled a few times will remove the limescale.

Soak burned-on stains in enamel pans in salted water overnight then boil the liquid the following day and watch the stains disappear.

Put candles in the fridge or freezer before lighting them – the coldness prolongs their burning life.

To prevent halved avocados from turning brown, refrigerate them flesh side down in a bowl of water into which you have squeezed some lemon juice. They will keep for several days.

To preserve the taste of freshly baked cookies and brownies, place a slice of bread in the storage container. The moisture from the bread keeps the cookies soft.

To lift stubborn food stains like burned milk in a pan, sprinkle on some bicarbonate of soda, add enough water to cover and leave it for a couple of hours.

To remove the smell of garlic or onion on a chopping board, sprinkle it with table salt. Cut a lemon or lime into quarters, using them to rub the salt into the board while squeezing the juice onto the board as you go. Let the board sit for two to three minutes and then wipe it clean with a damp cloth.

Chalk is a moisture absorber so to slow down tarnishing, tie up a few pieces in cheesecloth and store them with your good silver.

Use reusable food containers to make your own salads to bring into work – all those plastic salad bowls soon add up to a lot of money and packaging waste, which often can't be recycled.

Rinsing lettuce leaves in lemon juice will keep them fresh for an extra few days.

Avoid buying and using disposable plastic or paper cups, plates, cutlery and napkins for picnics. It doesn't take too long to wash up a few plates and the environment will thank you for it.

To avoid soggy, unused vegetables in the fridge, peel and chop carrots, onions, etc., place them in an airtight container and freeze. When needed, just take out as much as is required and reseal.

Buy cauliflowers with all their leaves still on and leave them on while storing, as this stops them going brown.

One brown banana left in the fruit bowl can be added to a curry. It works well with vegetables or lentils and adds fruitiness without being a definite taste.

Put a piece of scrap paper in with the vegetables in the fridge drawer. Any moisture goes into the paper, not the vegetables or salad.

Add stale or leftover breakfast cereal crumbs from the bottom of the cereal box to the ingredients in the bread maker while reducing the amount of flour accordingly. This adds texture to the bread, and even sweet breakfast cereal doesn't make the bread sweet.

Pesto can be frozen in teaspoonfuls in an ice-cube tray. When it's needed, defrost in a dish.

When baking, if you find you are short of eggs, substitute 1 tablespoon of white vinegar per egg – the results in cakes and muffins are impressive.

Mix yogurt with any overripe fruit, such as bananas and strawberries, pour into lolly moulds and freeze for delicious ice lollies.

Naan bread makes a great ready-made pizza base. Spread liberally with pizza sauce and any topping. Freeze for another day.

Fresh or long-life semi-skimmed milk can be frozen when too much has been bought and the family are away for a few days. It also means that there is always milk for a cup of tea on arrival home to an otherwise empty fridge.

An iceberg lettuce can be broken up and stored in the fridge in a bowl of cold water, allowing it to stay fresh and crispy for much longer.

Slice fresh bagels and freeze in airtight containers. When required, take them out of the freezer and put them directly in the toaster.

Wrap celery in foil and store in the fridge to keep it fresher for longer.

If apples have bruised areas, simply cut off and grate the remaining apple into salads or cut into wedges and eat as a snack.

Iced tea requires only half as much sugar if sweetened when hot than when cold.

Hold a day-old loaf of bread briefly under a running cold tap. After a good shake, pop in a hot oven for about ten minutes and it will be as soft and crusty as freshly baked bread.

To make an instant crouton mix, cut any leftover bread into cubes, toss in olive oil and a little garlic, herbs and chilli powder, freeze on a tray and transfer into bags or boxes when frozen. These can then be shallow-fried or baked in the oven and added to any soup or salad.

Milk frequently sticks to the pan when it is being boiled. To prevent this, rinse the pan in hot water before heating.

To bake a potato in half the usual time, stick a metal skewer lengthways through the centre of the potato.

To keep the fizziness in an unfinished canned drink, put the end of a teaspoon in the can and the next day it will still be fizzy.

Swap butter packaged in plastic tubs for blocks of butter wrapped in paper. If you buy butter in plastic tubs because you prefer spreadable butter, simply store block butter outside the fridge for the same effect. Butter will keep as well in a cool, dry cupboard, especially when kept in a ceramic butter protector, and it spreads easily at room temperature. Some recipes require chilled butter but you can cut the required amount from the block and keep it in the fridge ahead of baking. Use any scrapings of butter left on the wrapper to grease cake tins when baking. The scrapings can even be used to apply fat to pans when frying ingredients such as eggs or garlic.

Challenge – Try an Evening Off-Grid

The idea of no electricity or gas or Wi-Fi for one evening may be horrifying to some, especially if you are addicted to the internet, but there is magic to be had in slowing down your evening.

Make wild cocktails

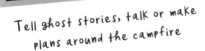

Tell ghost stories, talk or make plans around the campfire

Light candles

Cook on an open fire

Play card games

Have a bread and cheese night

IN THE WARDROBE
Slip into Something More Comfortable (and Sustainable)

Fast fashion takes a toll on the environment: with the multiple stages of manufacturing and transportation for just one garment, the carbon footprint of textile and clothing production is enormous. Even natural fabrics can be problematic: it takes over 5,000 gallons of water to produce enough cotton to create a T-shirt and a pair of jeans. In this chapter, discover ways to make your clothes last, make more informed choices about the clothing items that you purchase and embrace slow fashion.

How to Make Your Clothes Last

Many of us have bought into fast fashion in recent years, but now that its negative aspects have been made public, it's time to make a stand. Here are the key things when buying and caring for clothing to ensure it will last.

Check the seams – it's not advisable to pull at the seams of an item you have yet to purchase but instead take a close look at the seams and look for loose threads as this is a clear indicator that something isn't properly finished and is therefore likely to fall apart after a couple of wears.

See the light – hold up the items to the light and see how sheer they are. The general rule is: the finer the fabric, the shorter the lifespan.

Check for selvedge – the amount of fabric turned over at the hem. Look for generous selvedge so that items can be taken out or lengthened as body shapes often change over the years.

Check the fabric composition – items made from synthetic man-made fabrics, such as polyester, may last longer but the fibres that they shed during washing contribute to the pollution of the oceans. The other negative is that they aren't great against your skin, especially when you sweat, whereas natural fibres allow your skin to breathe.

Wash items less – it's not unhygienic to wash clothes less. Use a clothes brush on jumpers and woollen suits.

Be extra careful when washing delicate items by putting them in separate fabric bags. Placing your items in pillowcases and knotting them closed works just as well.

Wear a slip underneath a dress or skirt so that you don't have to wash them as regularly.

Economy wash – items that must be washed regularly should clean just as well on an economy wash, which uses less electricity and water.

Store items properly – clothes that are scrunched up and wedged into drawers and cupboards are unlikely to be worn or last well. Fold or roll smaller items and store them upright in drawers so you can see them all at once. More precious items need to be on wood or fabric hangers.

You will need

A single duvet cover

A wooden hanger

Coloured chalk

Scissors

Pins

Sewing machine
and thread

MAKE A GARMENT BAG OUT OF AN OLD SINGLE DUVET COVER

With something this simple to make, you can store your garments and transport them without the risk of damage.

Method

Begin by turning your single duvet cover inside out and lying it flat on a clean floor or work surface (if you have one big enough!).

Take out your item of clothing from the wardrobe and lay it flat so that the hook of its hanger extends beyond the top edge of the duvet cover.

Draw a chalk line about 12 cm (5 in.) beyond your item of clothing at the base of the duvet cover. Put away your clothing item.

Cut or score a straight line where you have marked with chalk. Then fold over around 3 cm (1 in.) of this raw edge and pin into place. Hem with a running stitch.

Next cut a small hole at the top of your duvet cover for the hanger hook to poke through. Topstitch the raw edge to avoid fraying.

Now turn your duvet cover/garment bag the right way out and press with an iron.

Place your clothing item inside with the hanger poking out of the top.

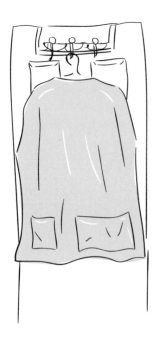

Use the leftover fabric to customize your garment bag with pockets for accessories or loops for belts so they don't go missing at the bottom of the cupboard! Or for extra protection of your items, add buttons or Velcro to the opening.

HOMEMADE MOTH BAGS

Another factor that can shorten the life of your favourite clothes is moths. If you can't carry off the holey look, then here's a way to eradicate these little pests with herbal power!

Makes three moth bags

You will need

A handful of dried lavender

A handful of dried cloves

A handful of dried sage

3 cotton handkerchiefs (or fabric remnants cut into approx. 30 cm (11 in.) squares)

Needle and thread

Ribbon or string

Method

With your hands mix together your herbs in a bowl.

Take a fistful of the herbs and place it into the centre of your first handkerchief.

Carefully bring the corners together and tie the ribbon or string so that the herbs are contained in a tight ball.

Stitch the knot in place so it's secure.

Place a moth bag in every drawer and inside your wardrobe. Squeeze occasionally to release the scent.

What To Do When the Moths Strike

Remove the garment from your wardrobe, place it in a sealed reusable plastic bag and pop it in the freezer. This will kill off any larvae or eggs that have taken up residence on your garment. Take it out after a couple of days and restore to room temperature. Then repeat the process and give it a wash as per the instructions.

Make Do and Mend

Here are some basic skills that only require a simple sewing kit.

SEW A BUTTON

You will need

Replacement button
Needle and thread
Scissors

Method

Start by looking closely at where the button was originally positioned. It's usually fairly easy as there will be strands of thread and pinpricks from the stitches.

Thread your needle and tie a knot to the end. Stitch from the inside of the garment to the front and secure the thread with one or two stitches, so you're not just relying on the strength of the knot to eventually hold the button.

Thread the needle through the button and begin to stitch the buttonholes. For a two-button hole, stitch up through one hole and down the other. For four holes, repeat the stitching so you have two parallel stitches.

When you have a good amount of stitches (around five to ten), take the thread underneath the button and wind it round the stitches a few times before sewing some stitches to the underside of the fabric to secure the stitching in place. Then trim the excess cotton.

Patch It

Patches have come a long way since leather or cloth patches were used to cover up threadbare elbows in jackets. There is an abundance of patches available, including hand-embroidered bees, retro Scout and Guide badges, tattoo styles and everything else you can think of, so when you've got a hole forming in your clothes that is simply too big to darn, there's no need for your heart to sink – see it as an opportunity to get creative!

You will need

A patch

Pins

A large needle

Yarn

Sewing scissors

Method

Position the patch and hold it in place with pins. Take your needle and thread a length of yarn onto it, then tie a knot to the end.

Thread the needle from the back of the fabric and through the edge of the patch.

Overstitch around the edge of the patch using small stitches.

Finish off by winding the needle back through a few stitches, pushing the needle through to the back of the fabric and sewing some tiny stitches to an area of undamaged fabric underneath the patch.

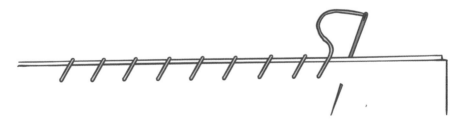

Darn It

Make holes vanish the traditional way! Darning is an art that may take a little time to master but it'll save you money and heartache when your favourite top has been chomped by moths.

You will need

Darning mushroom

A large needle

Yarn – either matching your item or contrasting if you want to make a feature of it

Sewing scissors

Method

Place the mushroom under the hole. Sew a couple of stitches about 5 mm (0.2 in.) from the hole then sew over those stitches to secure the thread.

Sew small running stitches around the perimeter of the hole, around 5 mm (0.2 in.) from the edge.

Stitch horizontally across the hole from one edge of the running stitches to the other.

Then carefully weave over and under the horizontal stitches vertically (see pictures).

When you have finished, secure with three stitches on top of each other on the perimeter of the circle that you originally sewed. Cut and neaten.

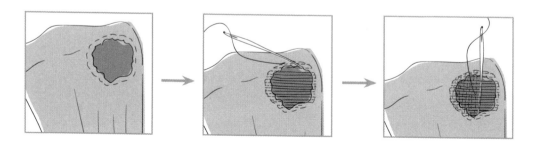

Place a few needles, pins and thread into an empty matchbox for an instant sewing kit.

Challenge – Alter and Customize Clothing

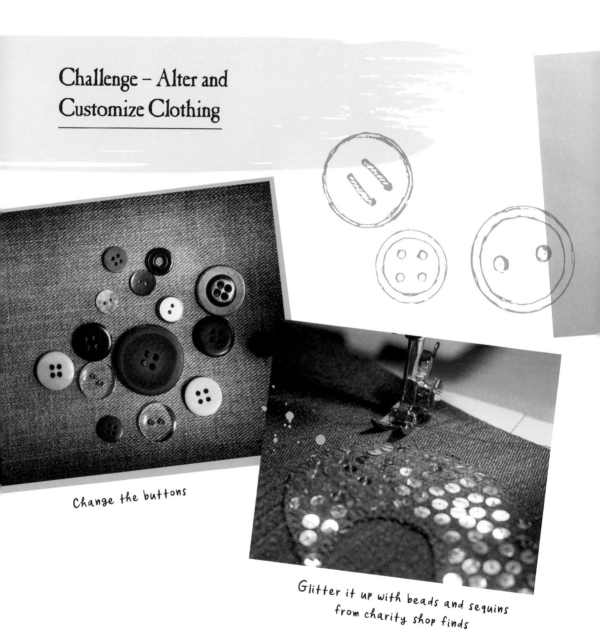

Change the buttons

Glitter it up with beads and sequins
from charity shop finds

Add pockets to a dress

Add a patch

Embroider some favourite words

DYEING WITH NATURAL, FORAGED MATERIALS

There's nothing more beautiful than the colours of nature, and one of the most exciting ways to capture these colours is through wild dyeing. It's also a cheap and fun way to breathe new life into clothes that you have grown tired of. It's best to use natural fabrics – cotton, wool and silk – for dyeing, as they will hold the colours better.

Anything can be used to create a natural dye, from onion skins and cabbage leaves to berries, bark and other foraged finds. There's a wonderful unpredictability to natural dyeing as the colours tend to lead to a few surprises – for example, onion skins will often yield a pinky hue and a red cabbage will produce an inky blue.

You will need

Bucket

Clothing made of natural fibres

Large old saucepan or cooking pot with a lid (you won't want to use it for cooking after this!)

Mordant (this is fixative, necessary to hold the colours. Alum is best and can be found in supermarkets as it's often used as a preservative, but if you want to go au naturel, lemon juice or white wine vinegar will do the job)

Rubber gloves

Apron

Your choice of non-poisonous plant for dyeing

Wooden spoon

Play safe with your choice of plant – don't use anything that is known to be poisonous or an irritant. Do your research first.

Method

Fill your bucket with cold water and place the item to be dyed in the water to soak for an hour.

Once the hour is up, fill an old saucepan or cooking pot with water and heat until it's on a rolling boil.

Add your mordant of choice. Ratios will vary but use 1 tsp of mordant per litre (1.75 pt) of water as a general guide. Stir until it dissolves.

Add the fabric and turn down the heat, place the lid on the pot and leave to simmer for two hours. Then remove from the heat and allow to cool.

Once cool, take out the fabric while wearing rubber gloves – just in case you are sensitive to the mordant. Rinse the fabric in cold running water and allow to dry on a washing line.

Now's the time to put on your apron! Next, create the dye by adding your plant material to the cleaned pot and enough water to cover the plants. Add your prepared fabric and slowly bring the water to the boil. Once boiled, cover and simmer for an hour, stirring occasionally with a wooden spoon and checking the colour every so often by lifting the fabric. Remember the shade will be significantly paler once the fabric has dried.

When you are happy with the colour, turn off the heat and allow the fabric to soak in the dye until cool.

Take out your fabric and rinse in cold running water. Allow to dry.

Wash your hand-dyed items separately when washing for the first time, just in case the dye hasn't set sufficiently.

Natural dyes

beetroot

carrot

blueberries

coffee

red cabbage

spinach

turmeric

onion skins

Make Your Own Bag for Life with a T-Shirt

With just a few strategic snips, you can make a stylish – not to mention economical and eco-friendly – tote bag out of an old T-shirt.

You will need

Cotton T-shirt
Scissors
Ruler

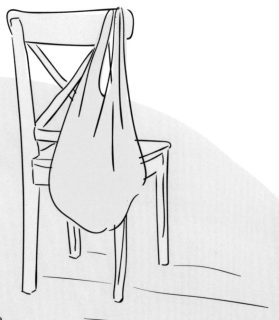

Method

Place the T-shirt flat on a work surface and cut off the sleeves along the shoulder seams.

Turn the T-shirt inside out and place it on the work surface with the bottom seam closest to you. Arrange the bottom edges so they overlap neatly.

Make one vertical cut down each side seam around 5 cm (2 in.) deep. Then cut vertical slits of the same depth all the way along the bottom of the t-shirt. You can use a ruler to keep your cuts even.

Working from one side to the other, knot each set of cuts together. You can double knot to create a secure base for your bag if you would like.

Turn your new tote bag right side out, and it's ready to use!

Quick Eco-Thrifty Wardrobe Tips

Remove winter salt stains from shoes by wiping with a cloth dampened in a vinegar solution. Use one part vinegar to six parts water.

Restore old shoes by rubbing a sliced raw potato onto the leather. Polish them with a cloth and watch them gleam.

Another way to restore the shine on leather shoes is to apply a dash of vegetable oil. Use a damp cloth to remove any dirt, then run a soft cloth with a drop of oil over the surface to (literally) add polish.

Don't throw away a garment because the zip seems stuck fast – rub the metal teeth with a pencil lead and now you should be able to ease it open.

Turn garments (especially corduroy) inside out before washing. This prevents items such as denim, black jeans or T-shirts with logos fading and also helps keep your clothes fluff-free on the outside.

To remove dried bloodstains from clothing, dampen the offending area with cold water, rub with a bar of natural soap, create a lather and then work the lather into the fabric. Rinse with cold water. Sometimes the process will have to be repeated, but this is a fail-safe method to restore fabrics to their former glory.

Faded colours? Try rinsing your clothes in water with some vinegar. This helps to get rid of the dulling effect of washing powder residue that can build up within the fabric.

If you have chewing gum on an item of clothing, place the garment into a reusable plastic bag and place in the freezer overnight. You can then scrape off as much gum as possible, rub in a little white vinegar and wash as normal.

Add a teaspoon of pepper to a colour wash to keep colours bright and prevent runs.

Most clothing can be reinforced in weak places like elbows, the crotch of trousers or any other part which bears a lot of strain or gets rubbed. Any lightweight material can be used, thus ensuring garments last longer.

If the front of a blouse has become too tight, place a contrasting piece of fabric along the button band. Or if it has long sleeves, make them short and use the material left over for your button band.

A well-worn cardigan can be restored to form by lightly running a pumice stone across the surface to lift off any unsightly bobbles.

Prevent camisoles and sundresses slipping off hangers by wrapping the hanger ends with rubber bands.

To eliminate lipstick from an item of clothing, saturate the spot with hairspray, leave it for ten minutes, then dab with a damp cloth or sponge to remove. Wash as usual to clean out any residual stain and spray.

Stop tights from laddering once holed by dabbing the area with a touch of nail varnish.

If clothes are no longer wearable, cut them up and use them for rags and dishcloths, which can be used for washing-up, wiping down surfaces or even cleaning the car.

Sprinkle salt into sweaty trainers or summer shoes, leave overnight then shake out the residue for fresher footwear the next day.

If you have a pair of tall boots and don't want to pay for expensive boot supports, place an empty wine bottle in each boot – it'll do exactly the same job.

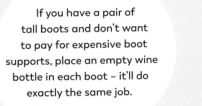

Conclusion

The ideas in this book are just the tip of the iceberg in terms of how you can reduce your expenditure while saving the planet.

The beauty of living a more eco-thrifty life is that it not only benefits the environment but also our own health and well-being, and that of future generations. We have learned that the world can't sustain current manufacturing processes or the throwaway approach to modern living, so it's up to everyone to be more mindful of their own impact and make changes – these can be big or small, and enjoyable too, as I hope this book has demonstrated.

Notes

Use these pages to add your own eco-thrifty ideas.

Image Credits

If you're interested in finding out more about our books,
find us on Facebook at **Summersdale Publishers**
and follow us on Twitter at **@Summersdale**.

www.summersdale.com